THE COMPLETE
ROBERT JOHNSON

By Woody Mann

OAK PUBLICATIONS
NEW YORK/LONDON/SYDNEY

COVER ILLUSTRATION BY LINDA GANUS
EDITED BY PETER PICKOW
MUSIC ENGRAVING BY MUSIC PEN, INC.

ORDER NO. OK 64965
US INTERNATIONAL STANDARD BOOK NUMBER: 0.8256.0314.5
UK INTERNATIONAL STANDARD BOOK NUMBER: 0.7119.2738.3

EXCLUSIVE DISTRIBUTORS:
MUSIC SALES CORPORATION
225 PARK AVENUE SOUTH, NEW YORK, NEW YORK 10003 USA
MUSIC SALES LIMITED
8/9 FRITH STREET, LONDON W1V 5TZ ENGLAND
MUSIC SALES PTY. LIMITED
120 ROTHSCHILD STREET, ROSEBERY, SYDNEY NSW 2018 AUSTRALIA

PRINTED IN THE UNITED STATES OF AMERICA BY
VICKS LITHOGRAPH AND PRINTING CORPORATION

TABLE OF CONTENTS

INTRODUCTION   4

A NOTE ON THE MUSIC AND TECHNIQUE   5

LEGEND OF TABLATURE SYMBOLS   8

THE TRANSCRIPTIONS   9

THE SONGS

   32–20 BLUES   21
   COME ON IN MY KITCHEN   66
   CROSSROAD BLUES   44
   DEAD SHRIMP BLUES   24
   DRUNKEN-HEARTED MAN   84
   FROM FOUR UNTIL LATE   92
   HELL HOUND ON MY TRAIL   71
   HONEYMOON BLUES   36
   I BELIEVE I'LL DUST MY BROOM   78
   IF I HAD POSSESSION OVER JUDGMENT DAY   49
   I'M A STEADY ROLLIN' MAN   27
   KINDHEARTED WOMAN BLUES   10
   LAST FAIR DEAL GONE DOWN   54
   LITTLE QUEEN OF SPADES   30
   LOVE IN VAIN   90
   MALTED MILK   82
   ME AND THE DEVIL BLUES   32
   MILKCOW'S CALF BLUES   59
   PHONOGRAPH BLUES   16
   PREACHIN' BLUES   68
   RAMBLIN' ON MY MIND   74
   STONES IN MY PASSWAY   56
   STOP BREAKIN' DOWN BLUES   62
   SWEET HOME CHICAGO   88
   TERRAPLANE BLUES   39
   THEY'RE RED HOT   94
   TRAVELING RIVERSIDE BLUES   64
   WALKIN' BLUES   52
   WHEN YOU GOT A GOOD FRIEND   86

INTRODUCTION

These twenty-nine songs represent the complete recordings of one of America's greatest musicians. Rather than attempting to analyze arrangements of his songs or providing a biography of his life, what follows is a presentation of the music of Robert Johnson in an uncut manner.

Very little is known about the man. The only information we have comes from sketchy remembrances of a few of his contemporaries and from the documented dates of these recordings. The professional life of a blues musician in the 1920s and 30s did not mean much to anyone, except perhaps to the record companies producing "race" records—and they did not bother to keep any biographical information on the artists. Fortunately, through the study of his surviving recordings, a more complete portrait emerges. The more questions that must be resolved in order to produce a transcription of a particular tune, the more that is revealed. These observations give us insight into Johnson's whole approach to his music, not just to a specific song.

His place in the lineage of American music and his influences on blues, rhythm and blues, and rock and roll has been widely conjectured in articles and books; and hypothetical profiles of the man have been portrayed by historians. This collection is about Robert Johnson's music, the only real facts we know. The transcriptions are one way of discovering his individuality and clarifying the subtleties in his music.

Like other blues artists, Robert Johnson was influenced by many of his contemporaries, and it can be shown that he borrowed from them freely. Sometimes he lifted entire arrangements from records or from other musicians. In his music one can hear the sounds of Son House, Charlie Patton, Hacksaw Harney, Blind Blake, Lonnie Johnson, and others. He took these influences and developed his unique style and sound. Each song has somewhat of a set arrangement, but it is the distinctive improvisation within the form that distinguishes his playing. When I first heard some of the recordings, I thought there were two people on the session. It seemed that there was complete independence between the vocal and the guitar and the two voices of the guitar itself. He was improvising, and yet each performance seemed very compositional—with a logical beginning, middle, and end to it.

There is no transcription that can fully capture the playing feeling of a performance—especially an improvised one. The subtleties of phrasing, tempo shifts, intonation, and rhythm cannot be notated exactly. I have tried throughout to be as faithful as possible to the recordings while avoiding the use of a lot of misleading complexities. Together with the rereleases of the original 78s, these transcriptions provide a good point to start looking between the lines and in helping to appreciate the beauty in his music.

When learning from the masters of the blues, the main lesson is evident by example: Develop an individual style of your own. This lesson is brilliantly demonstrated in the music of Robert Johnson.

A Note on the Music and Technique

The songs of Robert Johnson are in many different keys, encompassing a variety of guitar techniques and tunings in a mix of blues and dance tunes. With all his improvising ability, many of his recordings demonstrate that he had a specific set arrangement to certain tunes.

Upon close inspection, one finds some curiosities in his music. For instance, in his first recording session the guitar tunings and keys he used, in sequence, were: standard tuning in the key of A, dropped D tuning, standard tuning in E, open D tuning, standard tuning in E, open G tuning, and, finally, standard tuning A (perhaps he had more than one guitar). The songs "Ramblin' on My Mind" and "When You Got a Good Friend" are almost identical yet one is in open D tuning and the other is in standard tuning. The second takes are very similar except on "Phonograph Blues" and "Come On in My Kitchen," where they differ greatly from the first takes. In the songs "Terraplane Blues" and "Stones in My Passway," both in Spanish tuning and very much alike, the typical bass roll is deliberately and consistently different in each song. In "Stop Breakin' Down Blues" he has a bottleneck but does not use it until the last note. Many of the songs start off with guitar introductions in $\frac{6}{8}$ before falling into a regular $\frac{4}{4}$ meter—but even then, the time signatures may shift randomly throughout the tune. In the songs "Traveling Riverside Blues" and "If I Had Possession over Judgment Day," however, the meter changes are part of the form of each chorus. He seemed to favor the keys of A (in standard tuning) and open G ("Spanish") tuning, and there are strong similarities among the songs that are played in a specific key or tuning. Here is a breakdown of keys and tunings:

Key and Tuning	Song
A (standard)	Kindhearted Woman Blues
	Phonograph Blues
	32–20 Blues
	Dead Shrimp Blues
	I'm a Steady Rollin' Man
	Little Queen of Spades
	Me and the Devil Blues
	Honeymoon Blues
Open G (DGDGBD)	Terraplane Blues
	Crossroad Blues
	Walkin' Blues
	Last Fair Deal Gone Down
	If I Had Possession over Judgment Day
	Stones in My Passway
	Stop Breakin' Down Blues
	Traveling Riverside Blues
	Milkcow's Calf Blues
	Come On In My Kitchen
Open D (DADF♯AD)	Preachin' Blues
	Rambling on My Mind
	Hell Hound on My Trail
Drop D (DADGBE)	I Believe I'll Dust My Broom
	Malted Milk
	Drunken-hearted Man
E (standard)	When You Got a Good Friend
	Sweet Home Chicago
C (standard)	From Four until Late
	They're Red Hot
G (standard)	Love in Vain

In many of his tunes he would play a chord position but strike only a few notes in it. Since these positions are not generally too complex, the fingering has been left to the discretion of the player. Since all of his recordings in the key of A use similar positions, I have written out the following twelve-bar blues with chord diagrams, to help illustrate these songs. He is generally playing a bass line and a two-line treble accompaniment, so you will find the songs notated with up-stemmed notes designating notes to be played with the fingers of the picking hand and down-stemmed notes for those played with the thumb.

TWELVE-BAR BLUES IN A

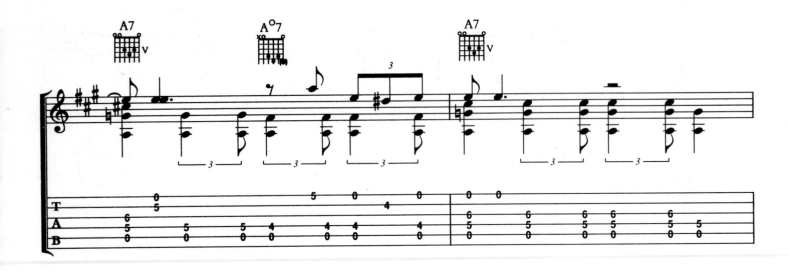

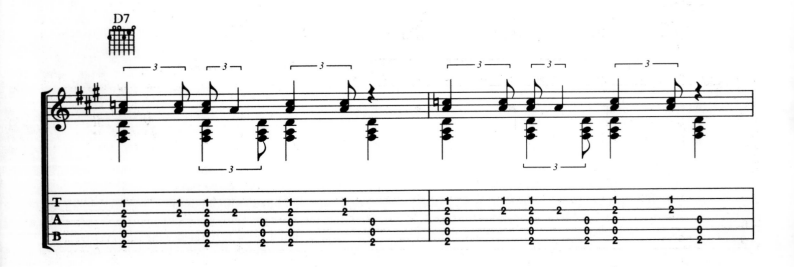

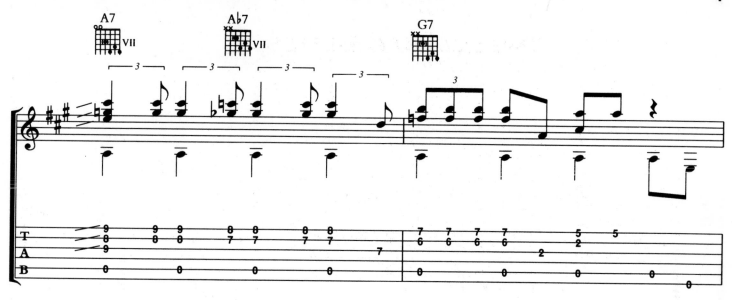

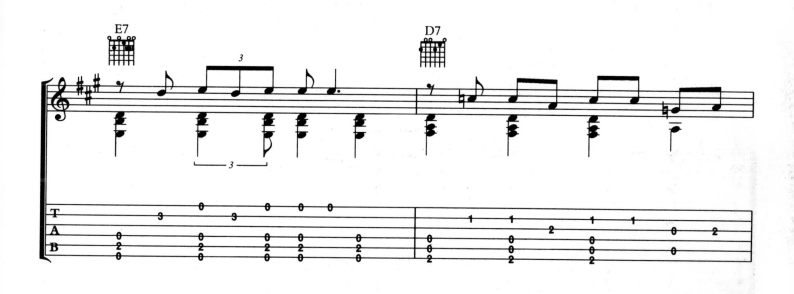

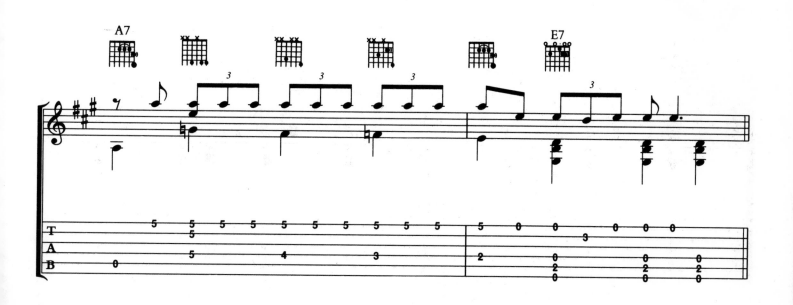

LEGEND OF TABLATURE SYMBOLS

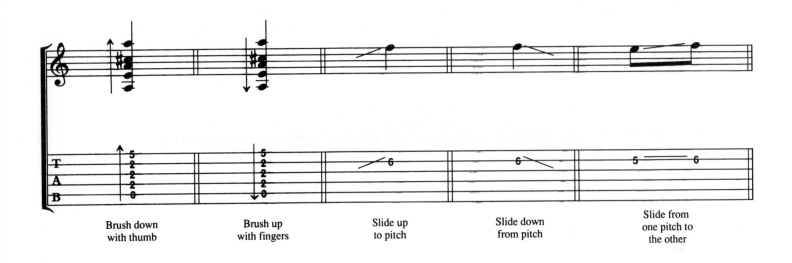

Brush down with thumb   Brush up with fingers   Slide up to pitch   Slide down from pitch   Slide from one pitch to the other

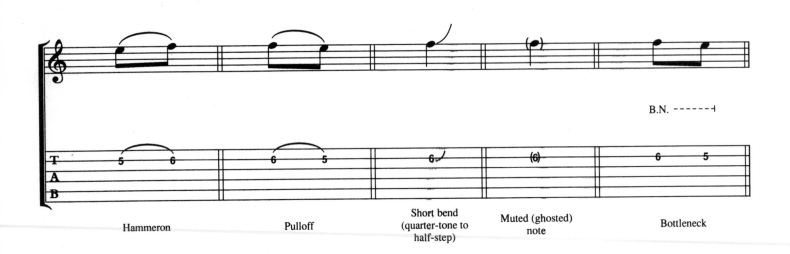

Hammeron   Pulloff   Short bend (quarter-tone to half-step)   Muted (ghosted) note   Bottleneck

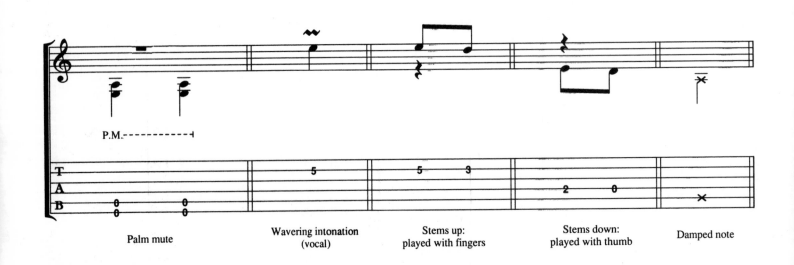

Palm mute   Wavering intonation (vocal)   Stems up: played with fingers   Stems down: played with thumb   Damped note

It is clear that Robert Johnson improvised within the form of each tune as he performed it. In most cases, the differences between each verse and the next are slight—so in general I wrote out only the introduction and the first verse. For some of the tunes, a second or third verse has been included if it introduced new material. Since his music is very free flowing, there are some verses that come out to be eleven, thirteen, or fourteen bars rather than the standard twelve. Also, within a given verse, there might be shifts in the meter to $\frac{5}{4}$ or $\frac{6}{4}$. In these cases I have notated all of these variations and included a second or third verse that illustrates the structure more clearly.

Sometimes the vocal line and the guitar part feel like they are in two different time signatures. In other songs it is simply the "feel" that differs. For instance, in "Last Fair Deal Gone Down" the vocal feels like it should be notated in $\frac{8}{8}$ or even $\frac{12}{8}$, but the guitar part and the overall feel of the piece is definitely $\frac{4}{4}$. In the interest of clarity, all of the songs have been notated in the basic time signatures of $\frac{4}{4}$, $\frac{5}{4}$, and $\frac{6}{4}$.

I have transposed all of the tunes to the guitar keys rather than presenting them in the concert keys of the vocal. For example, if he is playing a song in standard tuning in the key of A capoed on the second fret, you will find it written out in A—even though the concert key would be B. In open tunings the same is true. If he is in Spanish tuning (open G) capoed on the second fret, this would be notated in G—not A.

All of the tunes in this collection are available on Columbia's *Robert Johnson: The Complete Recordings*, which is part of their "Roots 'n' Blues" series. For related instructional material on country blues music, write to *Stefan Grossman's Guitar Workshop* (P.O. Box 802, Sparta, New Jersey 07871). A good source for vintage recordings is *Yazoo Records* (P.O. Box 810, Newton, New Jersey 07860). For further reading, the book *King of the Delta Blues: The Life and Music of Charlie Patton* (New Jersey Rock Chapel Press, 1988) by Steven Calt gives an accurate historical look at the blues scene in the twenties and thirties through the music of Charlie Patton.

KINDHEARTED WOMAN BLUES

Take 1

Introduction

ROBERT JOHNSON

Verse 1

I got a kind- heart-ed wom- an, do an-y-thing in his world for me,

I got a kind -

heart- ed wom- an,   do an-y-thing   in this world   for me

You break my heart ___ when you call _____ Mis- ter So - and- So's name __

Guitar break

PHONOGRAPH BLUES

Take 1

Introduction

ROBERT JOHNSON

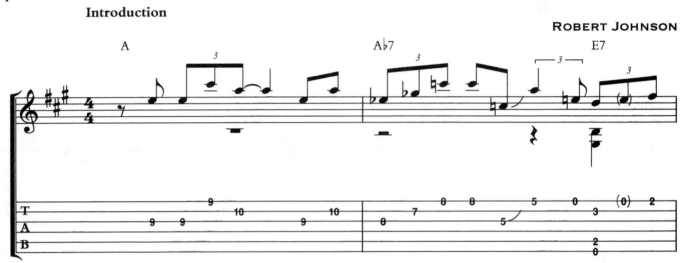

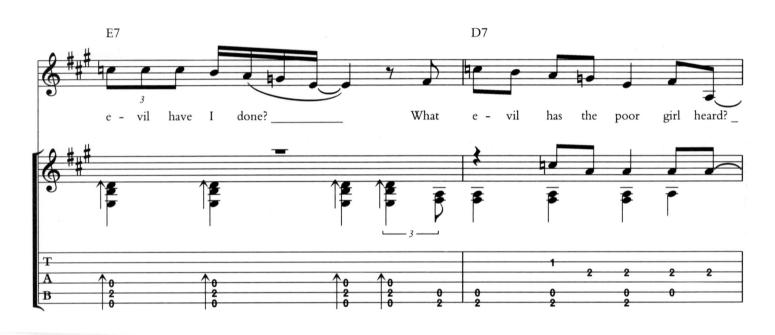

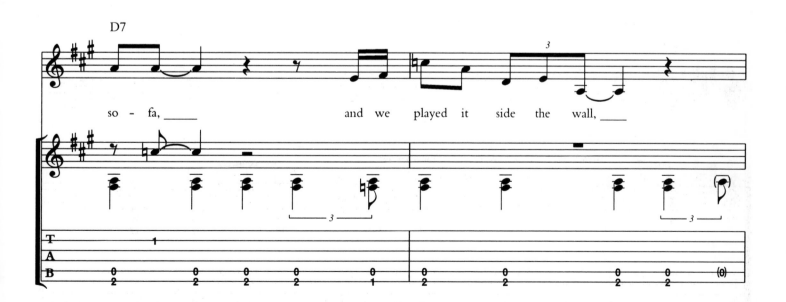

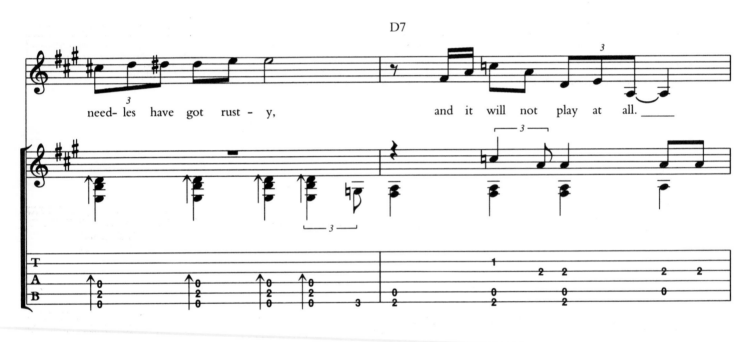

32–20 Blues

Introduction

ROBERT JOHNSON

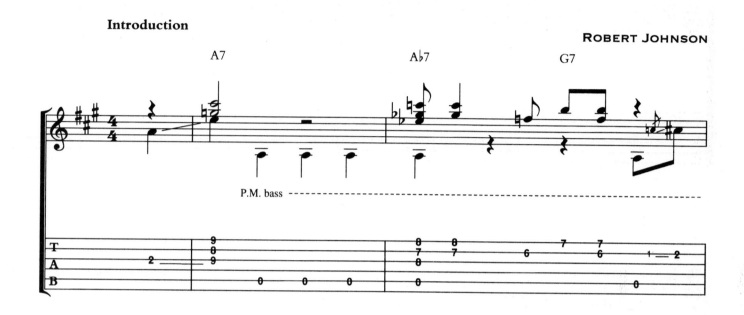

Verse 1

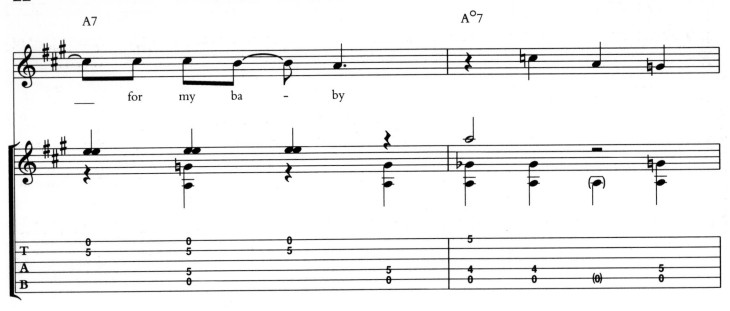

Dead Shrimp Blues

Robert Johnson

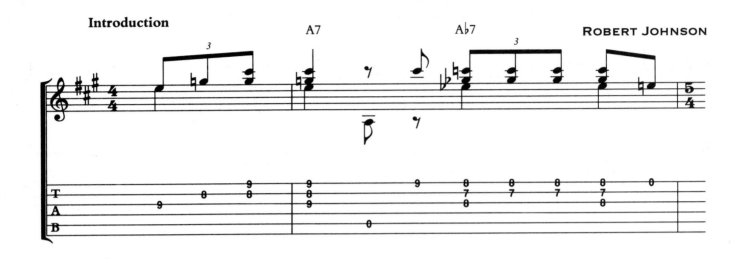

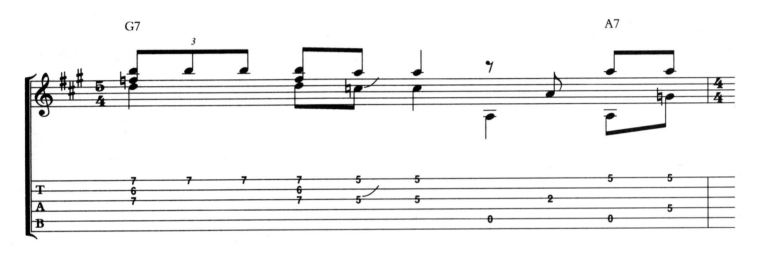

this morn-in', _____ and all my shrimp ____ was dead and gone __

I woke up

this morn-ing, ooh, _____ all my shrimp was dead and gone, ___

I'M A STEADY ROLLIN' MAN

ROBERT JOHNSON

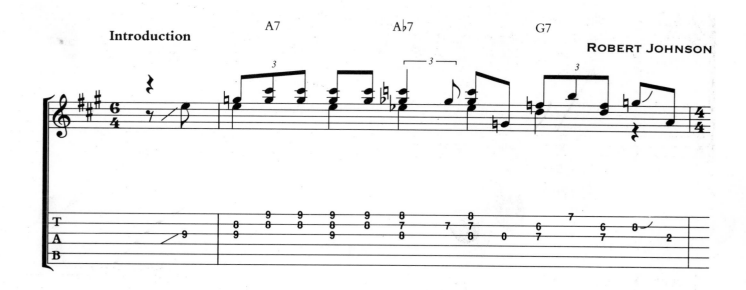

Well, I

have–n't got no sweet wom – an, __ mm __ boys, ___ to be roll - in' this - a way. ___

LITTLE QUEEN OF SPADES

ROBERT JOHNSON

ME AND THE DEVIL BLUES

Take 2

ROBERT JOHNSON

Verse 3

She say

you don't see why

that I will dog ___ her 'round, _

Spoken: Now baby, you know you ain't doing me right, now.

She say you don't see

why, ooh, __ that I will dog her 'round,

It must ____ ha' be that old e - vil spir - it ___

so deep down in the ground. _____

Honeymoon Blues

Robert Johnson

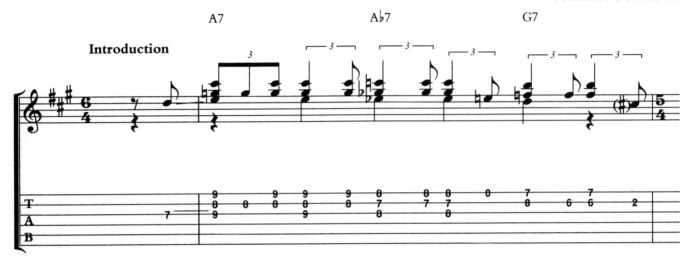

I wants a

litt - le sweet girl _____ that will do an - y - thing that I say _____

Terraplane Blues

Tuning: D G D G B D

ROBERT JOHNSON

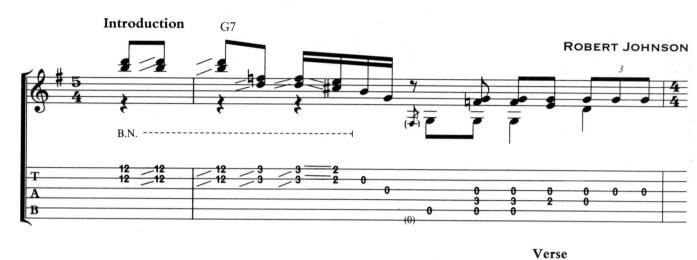

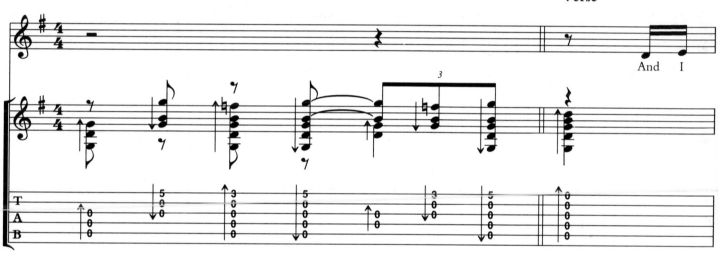

And I

feel so lone - some, __ you hear me when I moan, _____

Who's been driv - in' my

Ter - ra - plane __ for you since I've been gone? _____

B.N. ------

Middle Section
(Verse 5)

Now you know the coils __

__ ain't e - ven buzz - in' _____ lit- tle gen- er - a - tor won't get the spark,

Motor's in a bad con-di-tion, you got to have

these bat-ter-ies charged, __ I'm cry-in' Please, _____

please _____ don't do me wrong, _____

Who' been driv - in' my Ter - ra - plane now for ___

you ___ since I been gone? _____

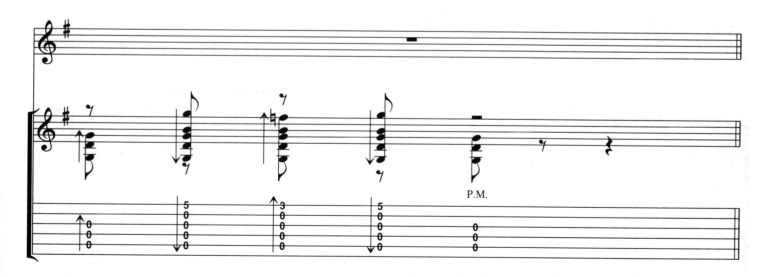

CROSSROAD BLUES

Take 2
Tuning: D G D G B D

ROBERT JOHNSON

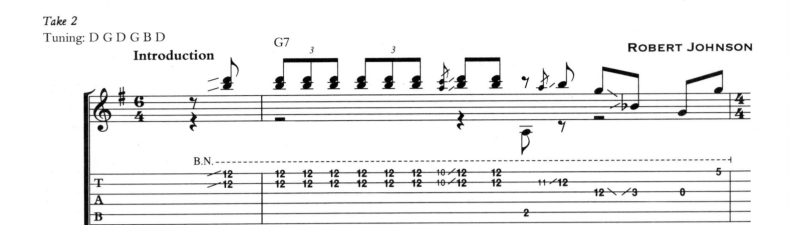

I went to the cross - road, _

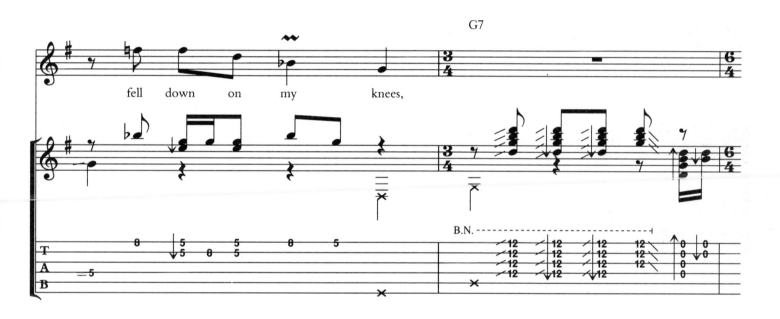

fell down on my knees,

I asked the Lord a - bove have mer -

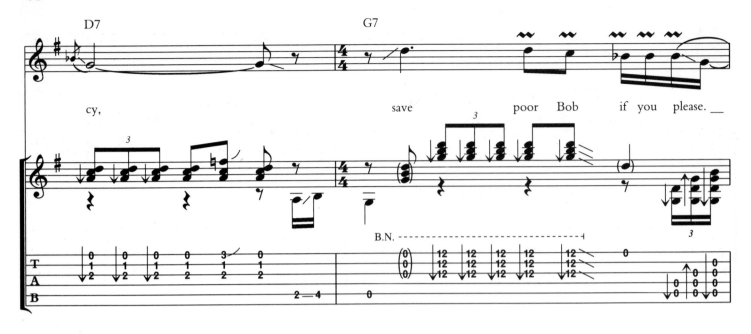

cy,   save   poor Bob   if you   please. __

Verse 2

Mm,

stand - ing   at the cross - road,   I   tried to   flag   a ____   ride, __

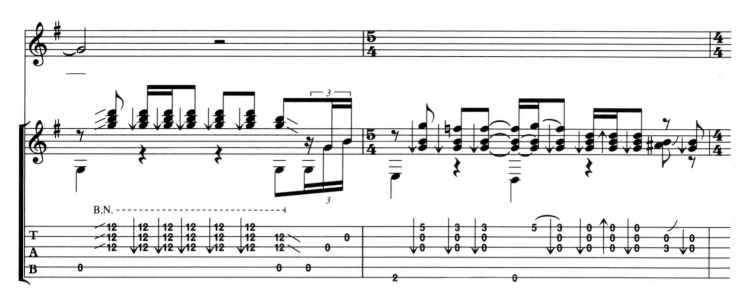

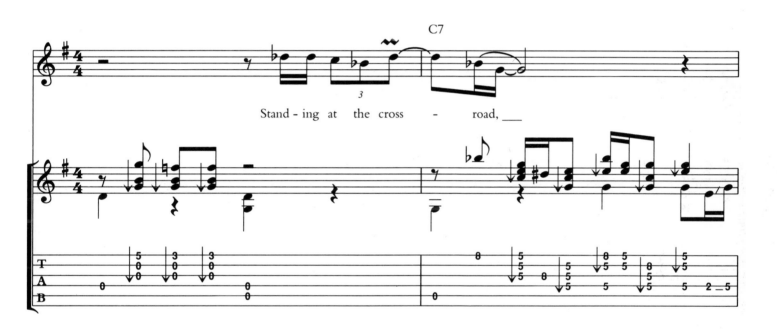

Stand - ing at the cross - road, ___

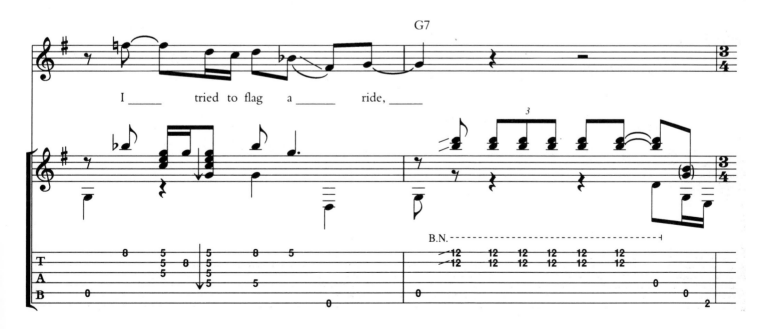

I ___ tried to flag a ___ ride, ___

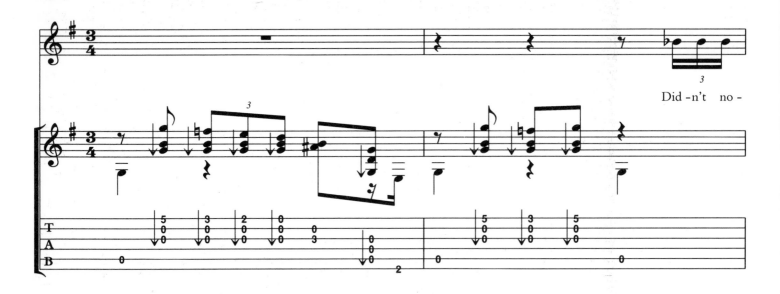

Did -n't no -

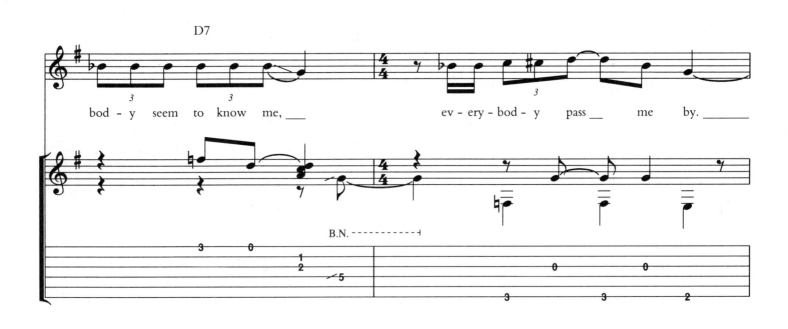

bod - y seem to know me, ___ ev - ery - bod - y pass __ me by. _____

If I Had Possession over Judgment Day

Tuning: D G D G B D

Introduction

ROBERT JOHNSON

Verse

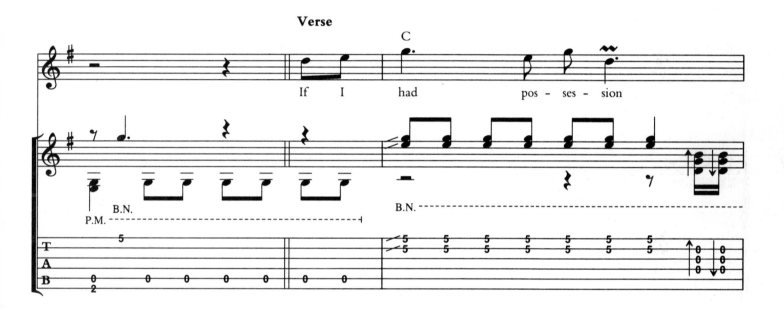

If I had pos-ses-sion

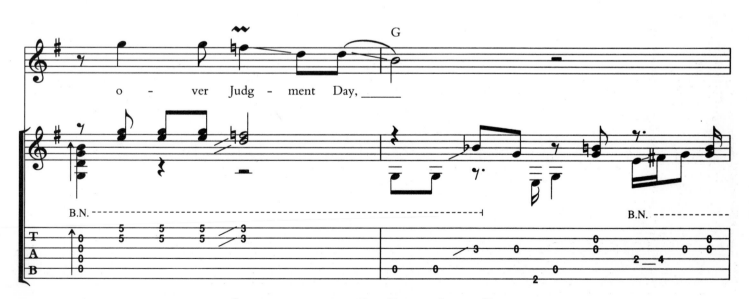

o- ver Judg- ment Day, _____

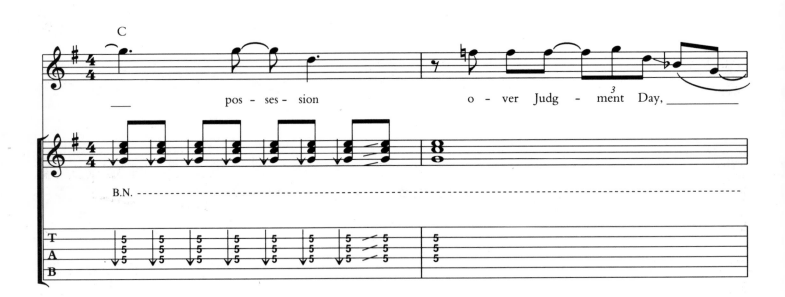

Lit – tle wom- an that I'm lov - in' would - n't ____ have no right to pray. ___

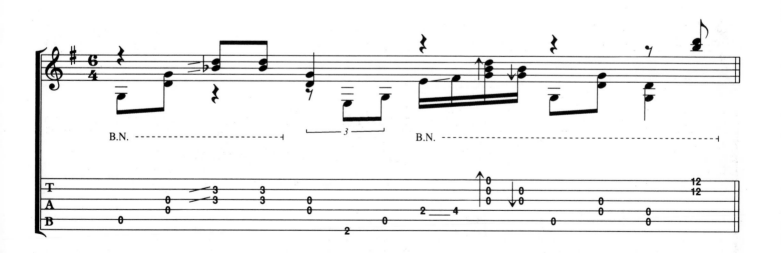

Walkin' Blues

Tuning: D G D G B D

Robert Johnson

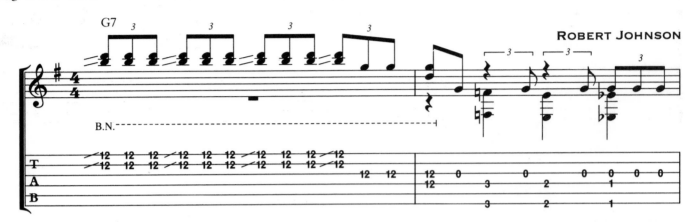

Verse

I woke ___ up this morn - in' _____

feel-in' round for my shoes,   Know by that, I got these   old walk-in' blues, Well

woke this morn-in' ____   feel 'round, _ ah, for my shoes, __

But you know _____ by that, I _____

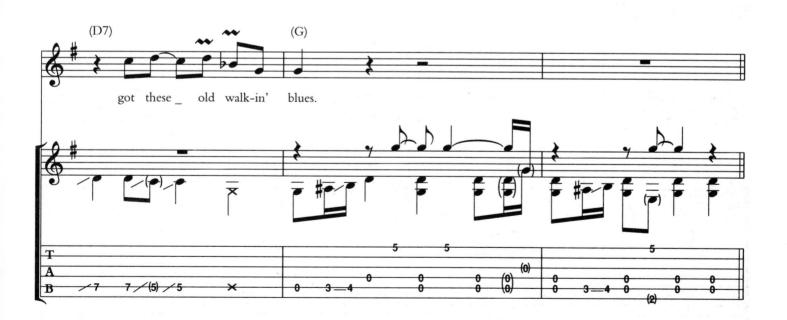

got these _ old walk-in' blues.

LAST FAIR DEAL GONE DOWN

Tuning: D G D G B D

ROBERT JOHNSON

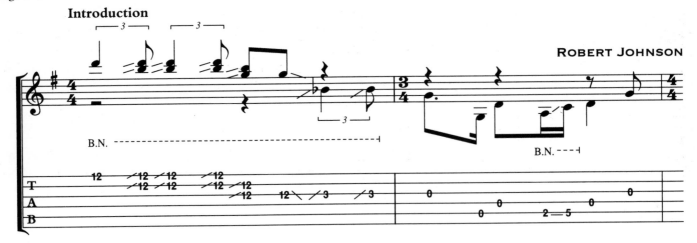

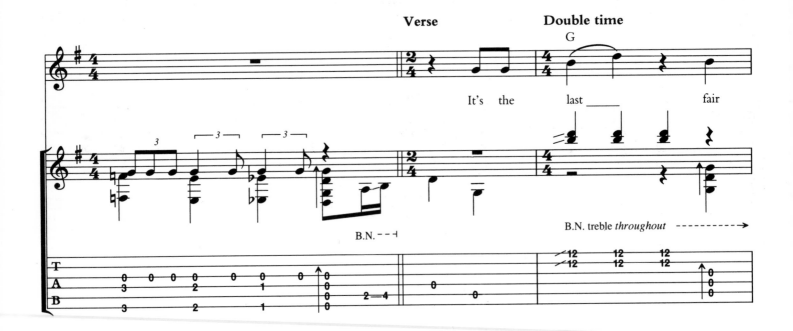

deal go - in' down, _____ It's the

last _____ fair _ deal go - in' down, good Lord, on that

Gulf - port Is - land Road.

Stones in My Passway

Tuning: D G D G B D

Robert Johnson

I got stones in my pass - way

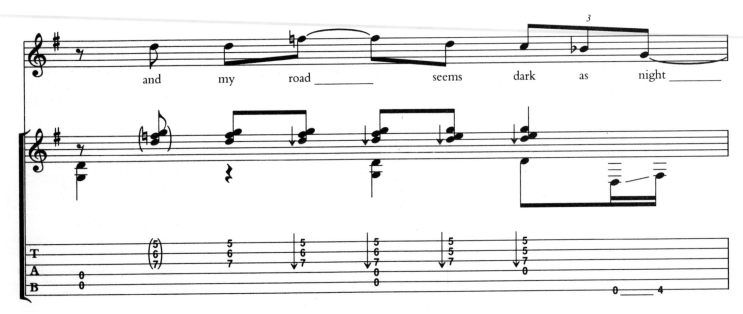

and my road _____ seems dark as night _____

I got stones   in my pass – way

and   my   road _____ seems   dark   as   night, _____

I have

pains   in   my   heart, _____   they   have   tak - en   my   ap - pe - tite.

MILKCOW'S CALF BLUES

Take 1
Tuning: D G D G B D

Introduction

ROBERT JOHNSON

what on _____ earth is wrong _____ with you _____

Ooh -

ee, milk - cow, _____ what on earth is wrong with you? ___

G7

Now you

have a lit- tle new calf, __ hoo - hoo, and your milk __ is turn-ing blue.

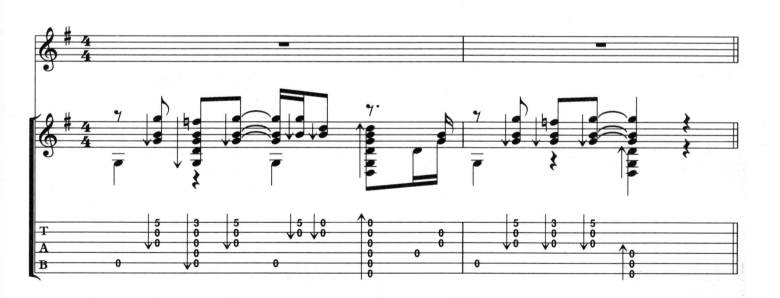

STOP BREAKIN' DOWN BLUES

Take 1
Tuning: D G D G B D

ROBERT JOHNSON

Introduction

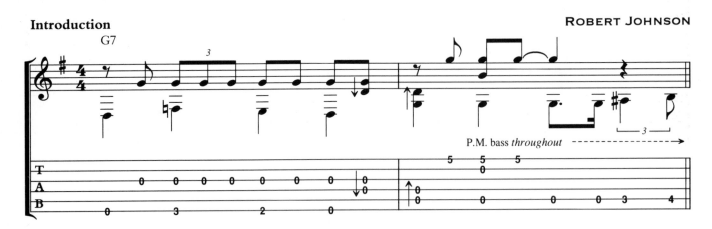

Verse

Ev-'ry time I'm walk-ing ____ down the street, ____

some pret-ty ma-ma start break-in' ____ down with me, Stop break-in'

Traveling Riverside Blues

Tuning:
D G D G B D

Introduction

ROBERT JOHNSON

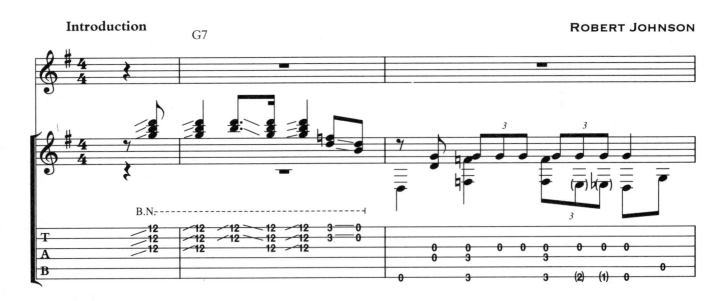

Verse

If your man ____ gets per - son - al, want to have your fun,

If your man __

Come On in My Kitchen

Take 1
Tuning: D G D G B D

Introduction

ROBERT JOHNSON

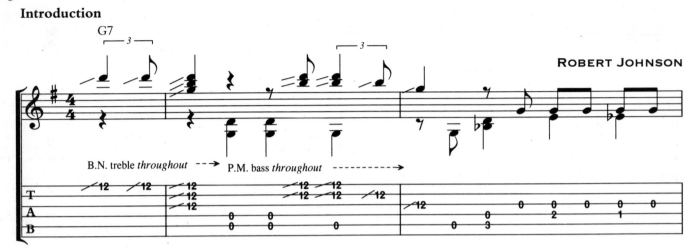

Verse

You bet - ter come on   in my kitch -

(D)   (G)   (D)

en,   Babe,   it   goin'   to   be   rain - in'   out - doors. ___

(G)

B.N.

PREACHIN' BLUES

Tuning: D A D F# A D

Introduction

ROBERT JOHNSON

I was up this morn-ing.

I got blues walk-ing like a man,

I was up this morn - ing,

my blues walk-ing like a man, _____

Wor-ried

blues,   give me   your right hand.

P.M. bass

HELL HOUND ON MY TRAIL

Tuning: D A D F♯ A D

Introduction

ROBERT JOHNSON

blues fall - ing down ___ like hail. ___

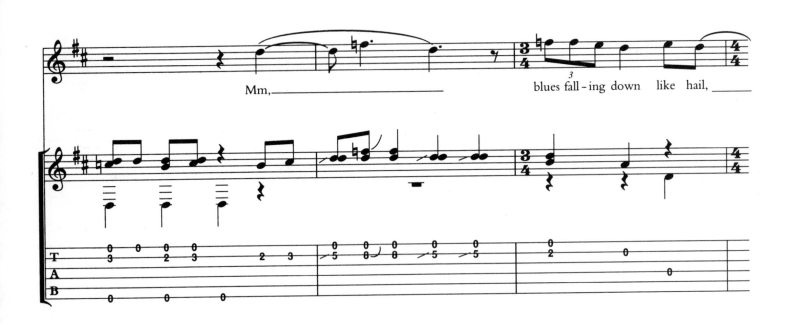

Mm, _____ blues fall - ing down like hail, ___

___ blues fall - ing down like hail, ___

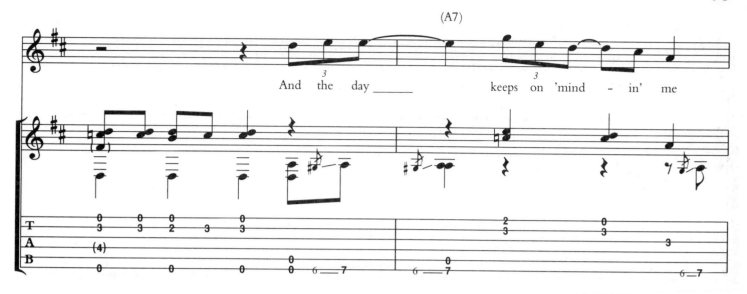

Ramblin' on My Mind

Take 1
Tuning: D A D F#A D

Introduction

ROBERT JOHNSON

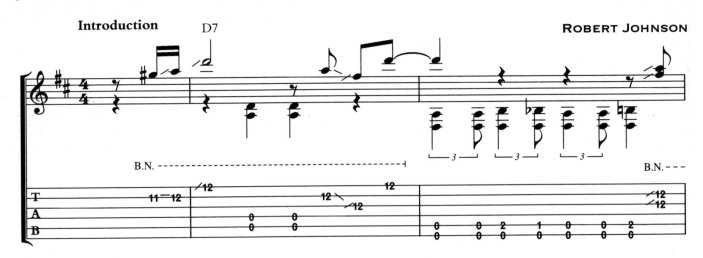

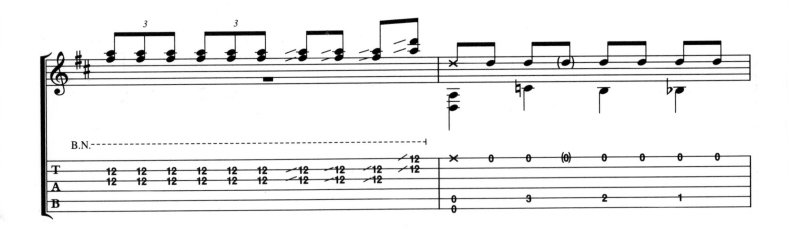

Verse 1

I got ram - blin', _ I got

P.M. bass throughout

ram - blin' on my mind, _____

G7

I got ram - blin', _____

D7

I got ram - blin' all on my mind, _____

Hate to leave my ba – by, _____ but she treats me so un – kind. __

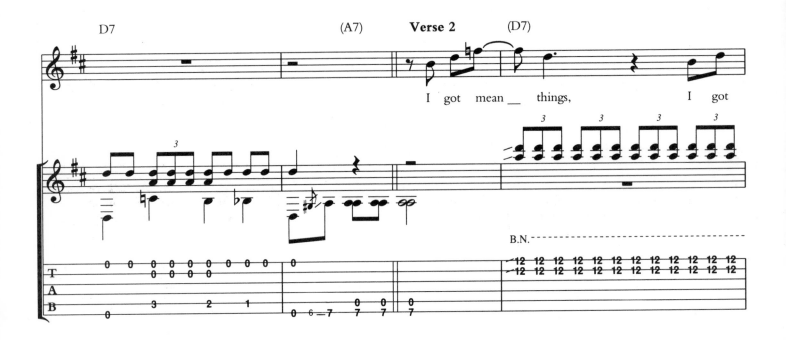

I got mean __ things, I got

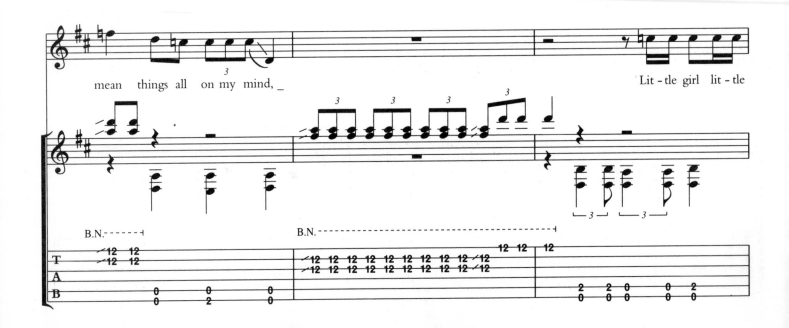

mean things all on my mind, _ Lit – tle girl lit – tle

girl, _____   I got mean __ things all on my mind, _____

Hate to leave you here, _ babe, __

but you treat me so un-kind. _____

I Believe I'll Dust My Broom

Tuning: D A D G B E

Robert Johnson

I be-lieve I'll dust my broom, _

Girl-friend, the black   man you been lov - in', __

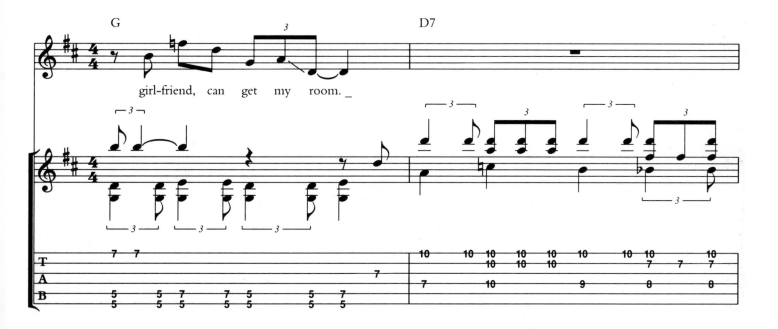

girl-friend, can get my room. _

Verse 2

I'm gon' write a let-ter, ___

tel - e - phone ___ ev-'ry town I know, __

I'm gon' write a let-ter, __

tel - e - phone ev-'ry town I know, _

If I can't find her in West Hel - e - na, _ she

must be in East Mon-roe _ I know. _

MALTED MILK

Tuning: D A D G B E

ROBERT JOHNSON

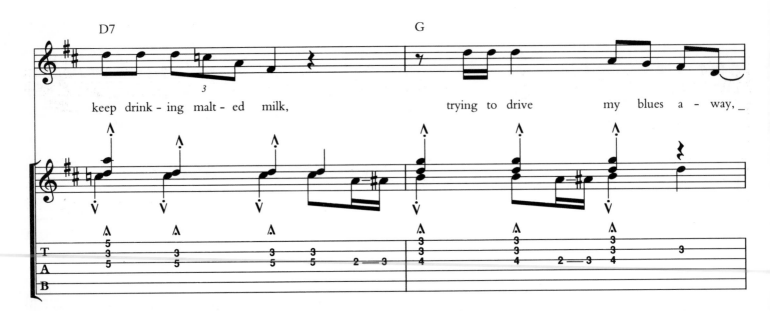

keep drink - ing malt - ed milk,   trying to drive   my blues a - way, ___

keep drink-ing malt-ed milk,   trying to drive my blues a - way, ___

Ba-by, you just as   wel-come to my lov - in'   as the

flow - ers is in May. ___

DRUNKEN-HEARTED MAN

Take 1
Tuning: D A D G B E

ROBERT JOHNSON

Introduction

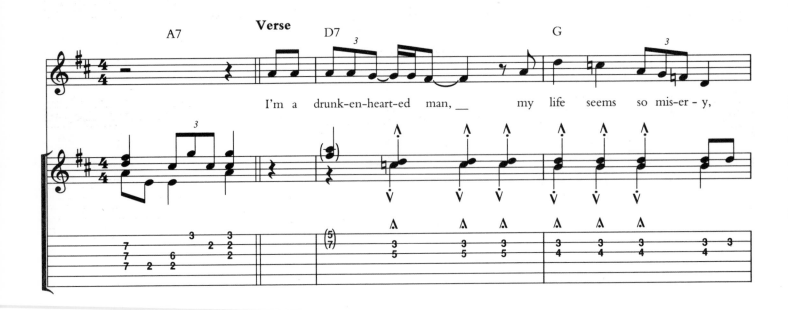

Verse

I'm a drunk-en-heart-ed man, __ my life seems so mis-er - y,

I'm the drunk-en-heart-ed man, __

my life seems __ so mis-er-y, ____

And if I could change __ my way of liv-in', ___ it would

mean so much _ to me. _____

When You Got a Good Friend

Robert Johnson

you got a good friend _ that will stay right by your side. _

Give her all (of) your spare time, _

love and treat her right. ___

SWEET HOME CHICAGO

Robert Johnson

ba – by don't you want _ to go? _

Back to the land ____ of Cal – i – for – nia ___ to (my)

sweet home _ Chi – ca – go? ___

Love in Vain

Take 1

Introduction

ROBERT JOHNSON

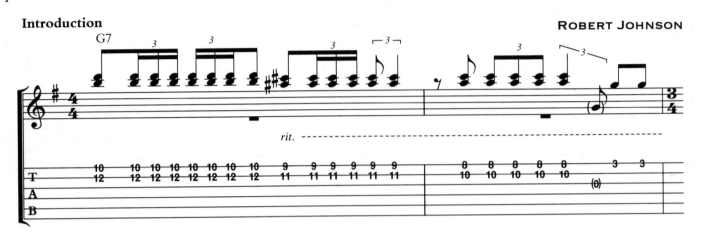

Verse

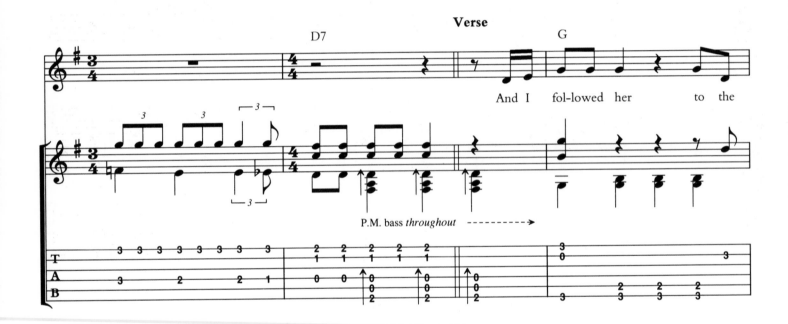

And I fol-lowed her to the sta-tion __ with a suit-case in my hand, _

Well it's hard to tell, _ it's hard to tell,

when all your love's in vain, _ All my love's in vain. ___

FROM FOUR UNTIL LATE

ROBERT JOHNSON

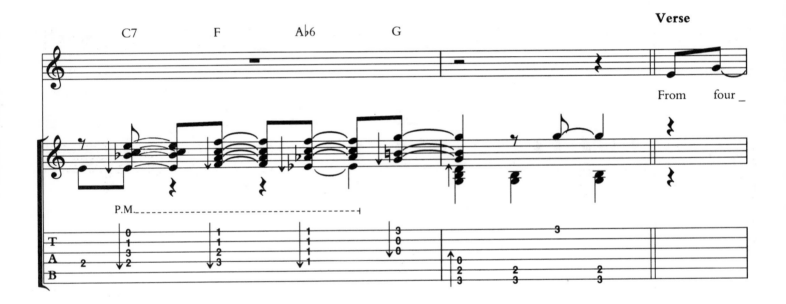

From four _

_ un-til late _____ I was wring-ing my hands _ and cryin',

From four ___ un – til late ___ I was wring - ing my hands ___ and cryin', ___

I be - lieve ___ to my soul ___ that your dad -

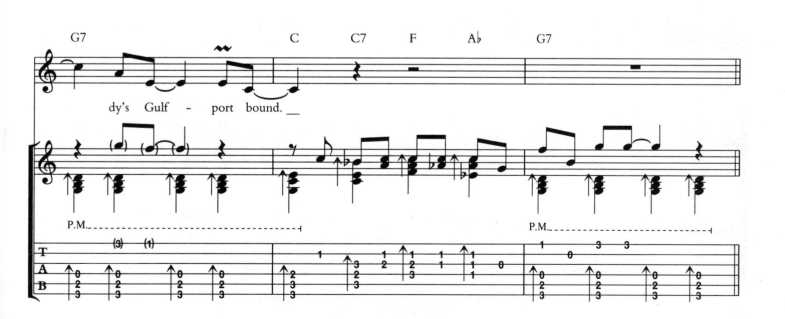

dy's Gulf – port bound. ___

They're Red Hot

ROBERT JOHNSON

Introduction

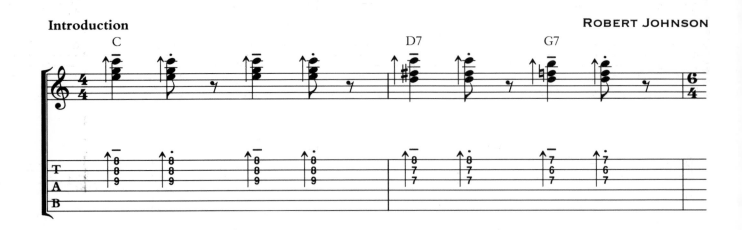

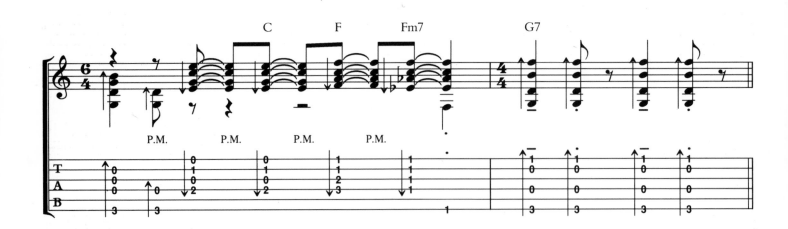

Verse

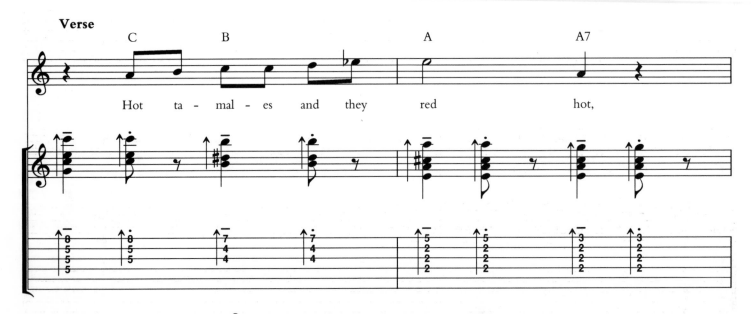

Hot ta-mal-es and they red hot,